TO: JORMEY Cualizares
you are perfectly perfect

Dean F. Scott

Mia London's
Perfectly Perfect Pajamas

by Dean F. Scott & Tasha N. Cook

illustrations & layout design by Shannon Freeman

Mia London Books
Roselle, New Jersey

Copyright © 2016 by Dean F. Scott & Tasha Cook

A Mia London Books Publication

All Rights Reserved

Published and Printed in the United States of America
Library of Congress Control Number: 2017919162
ISBN: 978-0-692-99928-8

Illustrations & layout design by Shannon Freeman
www.shannon-freeman.com

Dedicated To Our HUEtiful Girls!
Mia London, Kelsey Grace & Milan Lei
Always Remember "You Are PERFECTLY PERFECT!"

Acknowledgements:

Thank you to everyone who supported the Mia London Perfectly Perfect Pajama's Movement. We truly appreciate you!

Thank you to the most wonderful dad and our #1 supporter Dean Sr. You are our ROCK!

Justin, Danae, Symphony, Darnietta, MaMa and Grandma. Special thank you to Kiesha, Gary, Takeisha, Dawn, Ebony, Auntie Evon, Ashley, Auntie Loretta, Jacinta Perry, Evolving Diva Erica V. Walton & Val Pugh Love. Shannon, thank you for seeing our vision through your eyes and creating the most amazing illustrations we have ever seen.

- Dean F. Scott & Tasha N. Cook

Thank you, Mom, for always believing in me. You're the best second set of eyes an artist could ask for. My sister Grace for inspiring me, and for never complaining when I've asked you to model a million different poses. Dad, for blessing me with a love of art and continuing to watch over me from above. Grammy for pushing me so hard to pursue my dreams.

Tasha and Dean, words can't describe how thankful I am for the opportunity you gave me. I'm beyond grateful to be a part of something so beautiful and meaningful.

- Shannon Freeman

Mia London loved to go clothing shopping with her mommy.

Saturday was a very special shopping day. Mommy was going to let Mia choose her pajamas for Pajama Fun Day at school on Monday.

Mia was super excited.

The children's store was big, bright, colorful and stocked from ceiling to floor with all of the latest fashions.

There were fluffy, multi-colored tutus that looked like yummy, layered rainbow birthday cakes.

There were fancy dresses with Peter Pan collars, oversized buttons and bubble sleeves.

There were ruffles, rhinestones, and glitter.

Mia eagerly looked all around the pajama section.

She spotted pretty powder-pink nightgowns with graceful ballerinas.

She saw super-soft footie pajamas with pretty princesses and sparkly crowns.

She saw pajamas with jet-setting girls wearing big sunglasses and carrying international-stamped passports.

There were so many styles to choose. However, Mia didn't think any of the girls on the pajamas resembled her. None of the girls had hair or skin like hers.

Mia continued to search for her perfect pajamas.

Suddenly, Mia gasped with excitement.
She couldn't believe her eyes. She'd found the
most amazing pajama set, decorated with three beautiful
girls that had skin like hers in three shades of brown.

She loved how each girl wore a different outfit and hair styles that expressed their individual fashion style.

The pajama pants were decorated with pictures of vibrant lemon yellow and hot pink accessories such as makeup compacts, lipstick, and big fashion sunglasses.

Mia thought the set was absolutely incredible.
She'd found her perfectly perfect pajamas.

When Mia returned home from school on Pajama Fun Day,
she joyfully told her mommy about her wonderful day.

Everyone, including her teacher, had loved her pajamas. Many of the girls wanted a pair of their own.

Mia loved her perfect pajamas.

She adored them so much, she wore them to bed every night.

However, over time, her pajamas began to shrink smaller and smaller until Mia could no longer wear them.

Finally, Mommy and Mia returned to the clothing store to purchase a larger size. However, the saleslady told them the set was a sales item. She told them to check back for other styles later.

Mommy and Mia called the clothing store every week to see if another pajama set similar to Mia's perfectly perfect pajamas had come in.

Disappointingly, every week the saleslady told them no.

The news made Mia very sad.

So every night before bed, Mia would sit in her room at her art table and sketch images of little girls much like the ones on her perfect pajamas.

Mia would sketch and color until she would fall sound asleep at her art table.

One day when Mia returned home from school, she discovered a glittery pink box with a canary yellow bow sitting on her bed.

She wondered what could be inside the beautiful box.

To her surprise, there was a super cute purple and sky blue striped pajama set and brand new powder-pink shirt, both with a vibrant picture of three fairies with skin like her own.

Mia's heart filled with joy when she suddenly realized the three beautiful fairies were the pictures she had drawn.

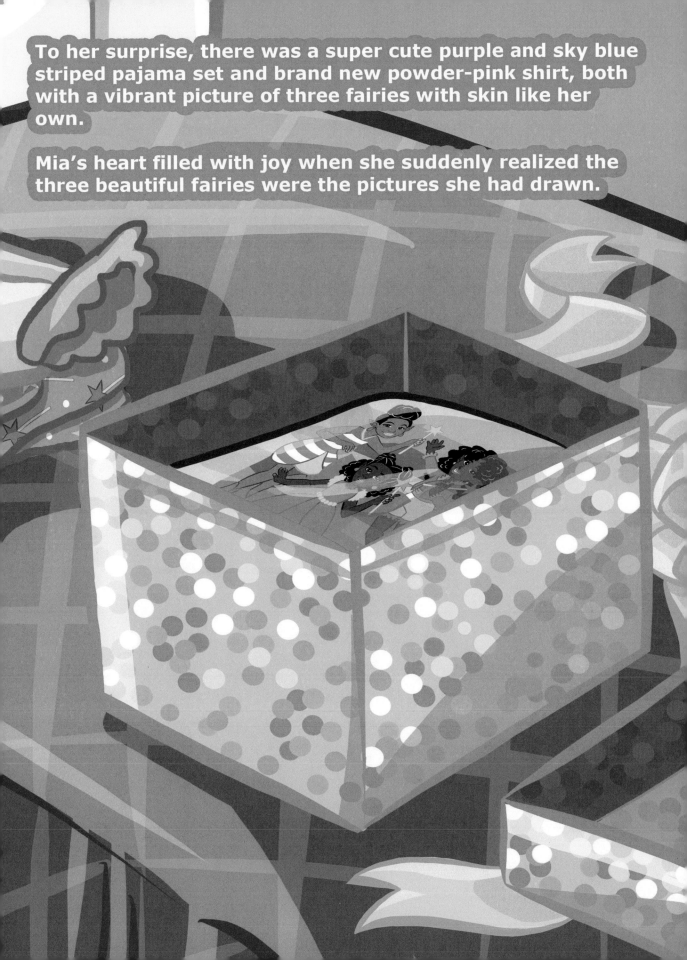

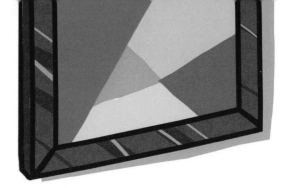

Mia ran into her mommy's office and gave her the biggest hug ever.

Mommy kissed Mia on her forehead. She promised Mia she would now always find pajamas and clothing with the images she'd drawn of beautiful brown girls in children's clothing stores.

Mia was delighted that she and every beautiful girl with hair and skin like her own could always have a pair of perfectly perfect pajamas and much more.

About the Authors

10-year-old Dean & mom Tasha are co-founders of Cocoa Mocha Kids (@CocoaMochaKids), an online social media resource page that reviews products for children of color. Dean & Tasha are also the creators of The Mia London"Perfectly Perfect Pajama" Collection, the first pajama collection for children of color, available at www.MiaLondonBooks.com

The mother & son author duo reside with their family in New Jersey.

About the Illustrator

Shannon Freeman is a New Jersey native and child-at-heart. She earned her BFA with honors in Illustration from the University of the Arts in Philadelphia. She works as both an in-house graphic designer and freelance illustrator. She's currently a member of the advisory committee for the graphic design elective at the John F. Scarpa Technical Education Center in Cumberland County.

Find more of her work online at www.shannon-freeman.com

Made in the USA
Middletown, DE
09 March 2019